Teen **ELI** Rea

The ELI Readers collection is a complete range of books and plays for readers of all ages, ranging from captivating contemporary stories to timeless classics. There are three series, each catering for a different age group; Young ELI Readers, Teen ELI Readers and Young Adult ELI Readers. The books are carefully edited and beautifully illustrated to capture the essence of the stories and plots. The readers are supplemented with 'Focus on' texts packed with background cultural information about the writers and their lives and times.

Maureen Simpson

In Search of a Missing Friend

Illustrated by Andrea Goroni

Teen ELI Readers

In Search of a Missing Friend
by Maureen Simpson
Activities by Sara Weiss
Illustrated by Andrea Goroni

ELI Readers
Founder and Series Editors
Paola Accattoli, Grazia Ancillani, Daniele Garbuglia (Art Director)

Eli Editorial Staff
Natalie Bayne

Eli Design Department
Sergio Elisei
Fabrizio Redaelli

Production Manager
Francesco Capitano

Photo credits
Shutterstock

The publisher would like to take this opportunity to thank Sarah Howell for her contribution to the development of the project

The publisher would like to take this opportunity to thank Lisa Kester Dodgson

Typeset in 13 / 18 pt Monotype Dante

Printed in Italy by Tecnostampa Recanati - ERT101.01
ISBN 978-88-536-0431-6

First edition: September 2009

www.elireaders.com

Contents

These icons indicate the parts of the story that are recorded

start ▶ **stop** ■

Characters

Camilla

Wills

Harry

flowers

Vocabulary

1 Label the picture with the words.

   flowers
   1 tree
   2 girl
   3 ducks
   4 lawn
   5 boy
   6 bench
   7 bush
   8 pond

8

2 Complete the text with the words.

> Gang   friend   ~~twins~~   a   parents   a

Harry and Camilla are ....._twins_........ . Wills is their best
(1)....................... . Their mother and father are wonderful
(2)....................... . Wills invents interesting things. He invented
(3)....................... Genius Kit and (4)....................... Missing Page
Finder. One day someone kidnaps Wills and the twins
hurry to rescue him. Read the story to find out how they
help their friend escape from the Black Hand (5).................... .

3 Circle the odd word out. Use a dictionary to help you.

shop (library) restaurant   sweet stall   supermarket
1 tree pond   forest   path   window
2 she   my   your   his   her
3 brother   sister   eats   friend   mother
4 first   second   six   third   fourth
5 tyre   homework   ride   bike   pedal

4 Match words to their definitions.

....._d_.... kidnap (v)
1 .... rescue (v)
2 .... invent (v)
3 .... missing (adj)
4 .... search (v)
5 .... gang (n)

a impossible to find
b create something totally new
c save someone from a bad situation
d take someone away by force
e look for something or someone
f an organized group of criminals

Chapter 1

Wills Disappears

▶2 It's a beautiful, sunny day in London. The twins are in the garden. Harry is mending* his bicycle and Camilla is busy with her favourite hobby, painting.

'Finished! Now my bike is ready. Camilla, let's go for a ride! Camilla! Camilla? Why are you so angry? What's wrong?'

'Look! They can't sit* still for one second! Now look what's happened!'

Suddenly, they hear a* bell ringing. They look to see where it's coming from. They see some bikes coming along the road. They're in* a hurry.

'Look! That's Wills' side-bike, ' says Harry.

'And he's not pedalling!' replies Camilla, 'Strange, very strange!'

mending repairing, fixing
sit still not move
a bell ringing a sound like ding, ding, ding
in a hurry going fast

'Hello!' yells* Harry. The bikes don't stop. They're going even faster. 'Wow! They're really in a hurry,' says Harry. 'Maybe they're escaping from something.'

Harry and Camilla are very worried. They run to Wills' house. When they open the door to his room, Harry exclaims, 'What a mess*!'

'Now it's a fact! The boys of the Black Hand Gang have kidnapped Wills!' says Camilla. Then she points* to a page of the newspaper and exclaims, 'Look at this!'

Complete the text with the words and find out what happened to Wills.

PRESENTATION OF NEW INVENTIONS, TODAY, AT THE GENIUS ACADEMY

Wills, the ..*winner*.. of last year's Genius Meeting, is presenting his latest (1) ..*i*............. .
It's a very special pen! 'It looks like a normal (2) *p*............',
says Wills, 'but inside there's a tiny (3) *c*............ that reads maths problems in your (4) *n*............, then it solves the (5) *p*............!' This is a very useful invention.

~~winner~~ computer problems notebook invention pen

---

yells speaks loudly, with a high voice
mess disaster
points to shows, indicates

11

'They want the pen! That's why they've kidnapped Wills!' exclaims Harry.

Camilla is very worried. 'But where are they now?' she asks.

'Maybe they're looking for the prototype* ... at the Genius Academy!'

'Let's get going!' says Camilla.

The twins take the Genius Kit before they leave. It's one of Wills' many inventions. But they can't open it. It has an anti-theft* device!

Do you think you're a *genius*?
Crack* the code to open the kit.

How many times is the word Genius written in the box below?

G	E	E	N	I	U	E	N	G
S	E	G	E	N	I	U	S	E
N	I	N	S	G	N	I	U	N
N	I	U	I	N	I	U	S	I
G	E	N	I	U	S	G	G	U
N	U	I	S	G	E	N	U	S

prototype model
crack the code decipher, work out
anti-theft device something to stop people stealing it

Harry and Camilla pedal towards the Genius Academy in Regent's Park, but Camilla is still worried. 'We'll never get there before they do,' she says. 'Don't worry, I know a shortcut* to get to Science Street,' replies Harry.

shortcut a shorter way to go somewhere

Follow Harry and find the way to the Genius Academy.

'We have to go straight on, then turn left. Next, turn right immediately. Then, go straight on until after the park. Turn right and go straight on to the Genius Academy', says Harry.

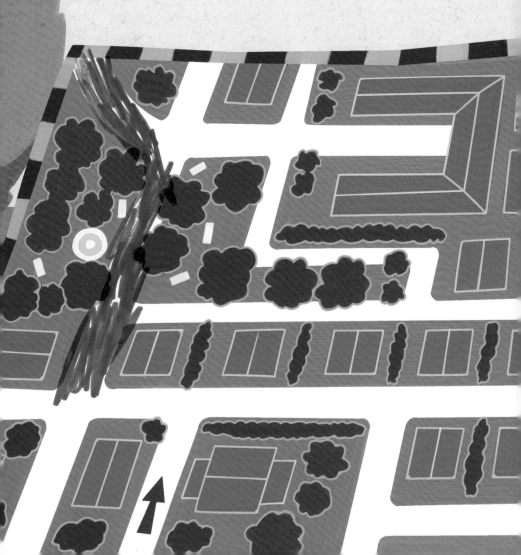

Harry describes Wills to the doorman, 'He's about this tall, a little chubby*, he has blond hair and wears glasses. Was he here?' But the doorman says, 'I see thousands of strange kids with strange inventions. They're all the same ... I can't remember your friend. You know, I have so many things to do. Look, I don't have time for you. I have to send out these letters today. I can't waste* time with you!'

chubby a little fat
waste time not use time well

Write the correct addresses on the doorman's letters.

Genius Way   Buckingham Palace
Magic Street   The Globe Theatre
Singer Street

1

Her Royal Highness

Queen Elizabeth

_____

_____

2

Mr Harry Potter

_____

_____

3

Mr William

Shakespeare

_____

_____

4

Miss Beyoncé

_____

_____

_____

5

Mr Albert Einstein

_____

_____

_____

After-reading Activities

Reading

1 Tick the sentences true (T) or false (F).

	T	F
Camilla's favourite hobby is dancing.	☐	☑
1 Wills is pedalling.	☐	☐
2 Harry and Camilla are worried.	☐	☐
3 Wills is with the twins.	☐	☐
4 Camilla and Harry leave the Genius Kit at home.	☐	☐
5 The twins cycle to the Genius Academy.	☐	☐
6 Harry describes Wills to the doorman.	☐	☐
7 The doorman remembers Wills.	☐	☐

Grammar

2 Complete the questions with What, Who, Why or Where. Then answer the questions.

....*Who*.... is Harry?

He's Camilla's brother.

1 .... are the twins?

....

2 .... are the twins worried?

....

3 .... is the Genius Kit?

....

4 .... do they take a shortcut?

....

5 .... do Camilla and Harry speak to at the Academy?

....

18

Grammar

3 Match the two parts of the sentence.

	[f] The weather is	**a**	to the Genius Academy
1	☐ Harry is mending	**b**	his bike
2	☐ Camilla and Harry ride their bikes	**c**	because someone has kidnapped him
3	☐ They see some bikes	**d**	coming along the road
4	☐ They can't find Wills	**e**	Wills' special pen
5	☐ Someone wants	~~f~~	good in London

Pre-reading Activities

Speaking

4 a Answer the questions. Discuss in pairs.

A Where are the twins, Camilla and Harry, going?

B Do you think they'll find Wills at Giant's Supermarket?

C Do you think the kids will buy anything?

4 b What about you?

What day of the week does your family go to the supermarket? What time of the day?

Prediction

5 Tick (✓) the items you think the twins will see in the supermarket. After you read, check your answers.

☐ fruit ☐ ear plugs

☐ bread ☐ ice-cream

☐ biscuits ☐ chocolate

☐ carrot juice ☐ a hair brush

☐ books

Chapter 2

Following Clues

▶3 When they leave the Genius Academy, Camilla says,

'The doorman is a liar*. Look at this clothes*
peg ... Wills is, or was, here!'

Harry takes a look at the clothes peg, 'There's
something written on it. "It's wood but it looks*
like burning rocks".

Maybe it's a message from Wills.' 'Your friend
was here a little while ago,' interrupts a boy, 'He
gave me some advice for my invention. Then he
went to Giant's.'

liar someone who doesn't tell the truth
clothes peg a clip to hang clothes
looks like seems / is similar to

**Complete with the correct word. Use a dictionary
to help you.**

- can
- packet
- carton
- piece
- loaf
- bottle
- ~~tin~~
- box
- bar
- jar

A .....*tin*..... of beans

1 A .... of biscuits

2 A .... of jam

3 A .... of milk

'Hello kids! Welcome to Giant's! How can I help?' yells the shopkeeper* to Harry and Camilla.

'H-h-hello!' respond Harry and Camilla, very surprised.

'Today's sale is gigantic! Buy Giant-carrot-juice, or a Giant-box-of-chocolates, inside each one there's a Giant-voucher* for a Giant-packet-of-biscuits! Are you interested? You're not interested, are you? Then try a Giant-quiz. Solve this Giant-quiz and you'll win a Giant-prize from Giant's!'

shopkeeper person who works in a shop
voucher coupon, a piece of paper you use to get something for free

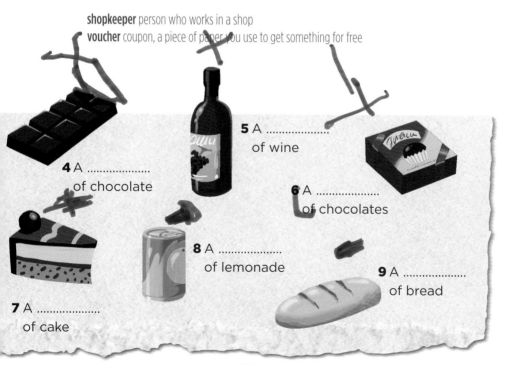

4 A .... of chocolate

5 A .... of wine

6 A .... of chocolates

7 A .... of cake

8 A .... of lemonade

9 A .... of bread

While Harry looks for traces of Wills, Camilla goes to the check-out* counter. The shopkeeper keeps* on talking, 'I assure you, Madam, we know all of our clients at Giant's. You are Mrs Stevenson. You come here every day between 12:00 and 12:15, then you go visit your friend Betty. Isn't that right?'

'That's right!' replies the surprised Mrs Stevenson.

While the shopkeeper talks, Harry finds a roll* of film. 'It looks exactly like the rolls of film that Wills uses. Maybe it's his!'

'Harry, what a bargain*!' exclaims Camilla, 'Giant's ear* plugs for dogs are really cheap. A real bargain! B-b-but what are you doing?'

'There was one of Wills' rolls of film in the supermarket. Thanks to Wills' photo-fax, we can immediately develop this roll,' explains Harry.

'Let me see it! Yes, it's one of his rolls. It's another clue*.'

check-out counter desk where you pay
keeps on continues
a roll of film in the past, people put film in a camera to take photos
bargain something cheap, for a low price
ear plugs what you put in your ears so you can't hear anything
clue an idea to find Wills

Look at the photos from Wills' camera. Work in pairs. What do you think happens next?

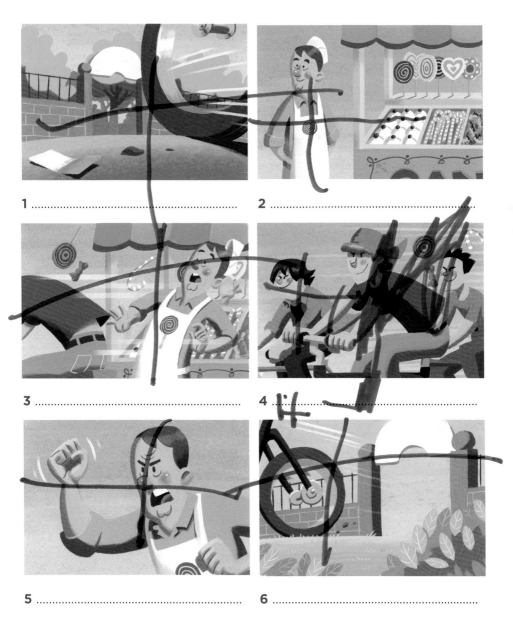

1 ....

2 ....

3 ....

4 ....

5 ....

6 ....

The twins run to the park. 'Haven't you seen them? Strange, very strange! They were here. And we have proof*!' says Camilla to the man at the sweet* stall.

'Here! This man in the photo is you, isn't it?' asks a very angry Harry. The man doesn't know what to say.

'Well, really ... I - I can't remember! My job is to sell sweets.'

Harry takes something from the man. What is it?

Find your way through the maze and write the letters you find on the way.

‒ ‒ ‒ ‒ ‒   ‒ ‒ ‒ ‒ ‒   ‒   ‒ ‒ ‒ ‒ ‒ ‒   ‒ ‒ ‒

proof evidence, something that shows what they say is true
sweet stall mobile shop that sells sweets

Harry looks at the clothes peg. 'There's a riddle*
on this clothes peg too. "You can find it in a
mine*. It's a hard stone that can cut."

'I don't understand,' says Camilla. 'Let's go to
the library.'

They hurry to the library, but they are too late.

'They aren't here any more!' says Harry angrily.

Then they hear another voice.

'If you're looking for someone I think I can help
you. I work here at the library and I love drawing.
I draw everybody who comes to borrow* a book.
Maybe my drawings can help you.'

riddle a mysterious message with a clue
mine place under the ground where you get coal, diamonds and gold
borrow a book take a book out of the library

'Wills likes drawing, too. He's the president of the Science Club. He's a nice kid, do you know him?' says the lady.

'B-b-but really, we were ...'

'He was here just a minute ago, with some other kids.

They looked at a book called *Kidnappings and Escapes* ...

'Can we borrow it?' Camilla interrupts.

'Sure, but you have to fill* out this form.'

'OK,' say the twins.

'Oh, look! There's a message!'

says Camilla.

'Let's read it!' says Harry.

Use a mirror to read this message.

I'm thorny on the outside,
sweet on the inside
and you can roast me.

fill **out** to complete

The twins take the book *Kidnappings and Escapes*.

Harry opens the book.'The middle pages are missing*!' he shouts.

'Now look at our bicycle tyres* ... they're completely flat. Someone let all the air out!' says Camilla.

Harry is furious, 'This isn't going to stop us! We're definitely going to find Wills!'

What can Harry and Camilla use to put air in their tyres? Find the words in the wordsearch. The rest of the letters will tell you.

- ☐ genius
- ☐ invention
- ☐ painting
- ☐ tyre
- ☐ bicycle
- ☐ page
- ☐ book
- ☐ pen
- ☐ Eddie
- ☐ rainbow
- ☐ Andy
- ☐ gang
- ☐ Harry

I	R	P	B	U	B
N	A	P	I	G	O
V	I	A	C	E	O
E	N	I	Y	N	K
N	B	N	C	I	P
T	O	T	L	U	A
I	W	I	E	S	G
O	H	N	D	M	E
N	A	G	D	A	T
P	R	A	I	N	Y
E	R	N	E	D	R
N	Y	G	P	Y	E

missing not present
tyre round, made of rubber, a bike needs two of these

After-reading Activities

Vocabulary

1 Complete the summary with the words.

~~go~~	asks	looks	goes	finds	talk	are	ride

The twins ....*go*.... into Giant's supermarket to look for Wills. The shopkeeper (1)................... if they (2)................... interested in the gigantic sale. While Harry (3)................... for clues about Wills, Camilla (4)................... to the checkout. Harry (5)................... one of Wills' rolls of film. They (6)................... to a man at the sweet stall.

Then the kids (7)................... their bikes to the library. They hope to find Wills.

Functions

2 For each of the sentences write where and why the speaker is speaking. Use the words in the 'where' and 'why' boxes to help you.

Sentences	Where?	Why?
Hello Kids!	*anywhere*	*greeting*
1 I'm sorry, we don't have your size.		
2 Can I borrow your book?		
3 That'll be £3.50, please.		
4 I'll have some juice, please.		
5 Where's the library?		

Where	Why
school / friend's home / library	~~greeting~~
shop / restaurant	asking for permission
street	apologizing
shop	asking for directions
restaurant	asking for payment
~~anywhere~~	ordering

3 Choose the correct response.

   When does Mrs Stevenson go to Giant's?

   A ☐ In the morning.
   B ☑ At lunchtime.
   C ☐ In the evening.

1 Who is the man in the photo?
   A ☐ He is the man in the park.
   B ☐ He is the twins' father.
   C ☐ He is the man in the library.

2 What club is Wills the president of?
   A ☐ Music Club.
   B ☐ ITC Club.
   C ☐ Science Club.

3 What happens to their bicycle tyres?
   A ☐ They are clean.
   B ☐ They're completely flat.
   C ☐ They are full of air.

Pre-reading Activity

Speaking

4 Answer the questions. Discuss in pairs.
   1 What is a riddle?
   2 Are you good at solving riddles?
   3 What do you think a 'Missing Page Finder' is?
   4 Where do you think Wills is?
   5 What do you think 'Do-It-Yourself Sounds' are?
   6 Where do you think Camilla and Harry will go in Chapter 3?

Chapter 3

Wills' Inventions

▶ 4 'Wills is a real genius! This missing-page-finder can find the missing pages!' Harry says, happy to have a friend like Wills.

'How does the missing-page-finder work?' asks Camilla.

'It knows all the pages that are in a ten* kilometre radius. It finds out which pages are missing and immediately prints* the missing pages!'

'Mmm, great, but it doesn't work that well. There are still some words missing,' says Camilla. 'A place close to nature, but full of people...' Camilla and Harry try to understand where Wills can be found.

ten kilometre radius ten kilometres in a circle around them
prints writes the pages on paper

Complete the page from the missing book with the missing words and discover where Wills is.

The Black .....*hand*..... Gang has (1).........................

Wills because they want his (2).........................

This pen can do (3).........................

The gang took (4)......................... to a

(5)......................... place.

It's close to nature, but full of people.

Wills   ~~hand~~

maths homework

secret   pen

kidnapped

'The kidnappers aren't very good. There are clues everywhere,' says Camilla.

'Wills is smarter* than his kidnappers. Maybe the riddles on the clothes pegs say where the hiding* place is. Let's read them again!' replies Harry.

Read the definitions and choose the correct words.

1 It's wood but it looks like burning rocks.

2 You can find it in a mine. It's a hard stone that can cut.

3 I'm thorny* on the outside, sweet on the inside and you can roast me.

- ☐ diamond
- ☐ gold
- ☐ chestnut
- ☐ coal
- ☐ oil
- ☐ rock

smarter more intelligent
hiding place unknown place where they took Wills
thorny has sharp needles, like a rose

'Hey! Is this your clothes peg?' asks a boy.

'Another riddle!' exclaims Harry. "Coal is east, diamonds are west, and I'm in the forest that loses its leaves."

'It's nice to have a friend like Wills, but sometimes I can't understand him,' says Camilla.

'Are you friends of Wills?' asks the boy.

'Do you know where he is?' asks Harry.

'No, I'm looking for him too. He has to mend this invention. It's called Do-It-Yourself-Sounds. It makes all kinds of sounds.

'You can't find Wills, but you have some clues. Mmm, coal, diamonds, chestnuts, a forest that loses its leaves... the place you're looking for is the park!' exclaims the little boy.

'Th-the park?' Harry and Camilla repeat together.

'Yes, look for him in the park. I'm very intuitive*, I never make a mistake.

intuitive has a feeling for things, good at guessing

How about you? Are you intuitive? Solve this.'

What time completes the series?

12:15

11:55

11:35

11:15

'Wills is in Regent's Park. Maybe that little boy is right. But there aren't any coal or diamond mines there,' says Harry. 'There's an old coal train and there's a baseball field in the shape of a diamond and there's even a forest!' replies Camilla.

'Maybe that's the solution, Harry. Let's read the directions on the map.'

Follow the instructions. Can you find Wills?

Take one step south, two steps east, one step north, one step west, one step north and one step west. Take one step north and two east and finally one step south.

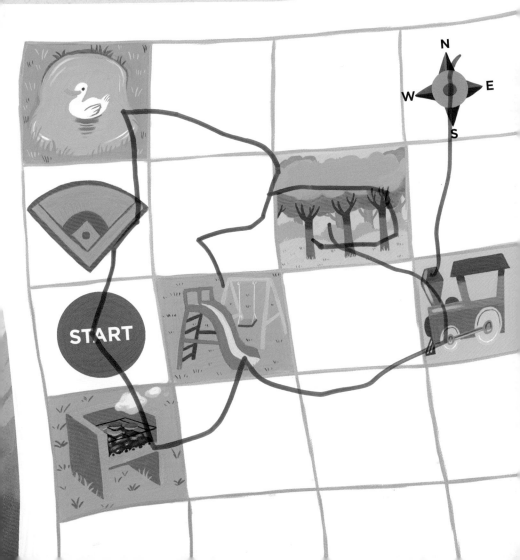

Vocabulary

1 Read chapter 3 to complete the sentences.

1 The Missing-page-finder can find the .... pages.

2 The kidnappers aren't very ....

3 Wills is .... than the kidnappers.

4 There are .... everywhere.

5 The Do-it-Yourselves Sounds invention makes all kinds of ....

6 The little boy thinks Wills is in the ....

7 Camilla and Harry decide to .... the directions on the map.

2 Match the phrases to their meanings.

    ☑ *b* Stop

1 ☐ No-Littering

2 ☐ Do not walk on the grass

3 ☐ No Parking

4 ☐ Park opens at 7:30am and closes at sunset

5 ☐ Ask to see the children's menu

a There are special meals for children.

b You must stop here.

c You cannot throw rubbish on the ground.

d The park is closed after dark.

e You cannot walk here.

f Parking is not permitted here.

3 Complete the sentences with the correct word.

I need to go to sleep now, I'm ...*tired*...... . (happy / interested / ~~tired~~)

1 Wills is a genius; he's extremely .... (short / thin / intelligent)

2 The page finder finds the .... pages (missing / prints / yellow)

3 Harry has a very .... bicycle. (fat / fast / sad)

4 There's a .... diamond in the park. (tennis / baseball / football)

5 The twins are .... about Wills. (special / funny / worried)

4 Write a short summary of the story so far.

Pre-reading Activities

Prediction

5 Tick (✓) which words you think the twins and Wills will use in the next chapter. After you read check your answers.

☐ forest   ☐ hiding place
☐ park   ☐ chewing gum
☐ ice-cream   ☐ balloon
☐ baby   ☐ ham
☐ orange   ☐ dog
☐ gang   ☐ apple
☐ bubble   ☐ police
☐ east   ☐ west
☐ north   ☐ chocolate
☐ water   ☐ house

6 Now use the words: tell your partner what you think will happen in the next chapter.

Chapter 4

Twins to the Rescue

▶ 5 'Two steps east...one south... Here we are!' 'Wills'
hiding place is the forest!!!' exclaim Harry and
Camilla together. 'The one that's in the north of
the park!'

'Eureka! We've solved the case!' yells Harry.

'Wait, now comes the hard part,' interrupts*
Camilla.

interrupts says while Harry is still talking

'Confess★ or else...'

'I've got no hiding place for the pen. It's very close to me.'

'That's Wills' voice,' whispers★ Harry. 'He's here, but how are we going to get him out? Have you got any ideas, Camilla? Camilla?!'

'Mmmm ... yummy! This thousand-tastes-chewing-gum is so good! It was in the Genius Kit, mmm ... now it tastes like ice-cream. Now it tastes like ham .... now it's chocolate.'

'Yuck! Disgusting★!' exclaims Harry looking at his sister. 'Thanks to your chewing-gum, I've got an idea!' exclaims Harry.

'Hey! Whose gun is that? Leave it alone!' says Camilla. 'Don't be afraid, sis★, it's a chewing-gum-gun.

Now give me your disgusting chewing-gum!'

'A chewing-gum-gun?' repeats Camilla.

---

confess or else tell us or we're going to do something to hurt you
whisper to speak in a low voice, not loud
disgusting gross, something that doesn't taste or look good
sis short for sister

'Sure! Loaded* with large doses* of chewing-gum, this gun shoots* a huge bubble* and ... filled with water becomes a huge water balloon!'

Tick (✓) the sentences true (T) or false (F) to find the hidden word.

		T	F
The gang's hiding place is in the lake.		☐ C	☑ B
1 The forest is north.		☐ A	☐ O
2 Thre's a pond in the park.		☐ L	☐ T
3 There are two boys in the gang.		☐ U	☐ L
4 The chewing-gum is like ice-cream and ham.		☐ O	☐ P
5 A baseball field is shaped like a star.		☐ K	☐ O
6 There's a train in the forest.		☐ N	☐ X

<u>B</u> _ _ _ _ _ _

---

loaded full
doses amounts, quantities
shoots lets out
bubble like a ball, full of air

'That's a perfect plan! Let's cut the rope that's holding the balloon and go into the shack* to free Wills. Then we can escape!' says an excited Camilla.

'Except there's one little problem...' says Harry.

'What's that?' asks Camilla.

'I can't remember which rope is holding the balloon.'

'Harry! You're always muddling* things up!' screams* Camilla.

'Maybe it's the red one. No, yes, I'm sure now. It's the yellow one.

'You're trapped*!' yells Harry, going into the shack.

'Hello! You're finally here!' exclaims Wills when he sees his two friends.

'B-but what's happening?' yells the leader of the gang. 'Eddie! Andy! Stop those two! Get Wills! He still has to tell us where the pen is!'

'Sure boss. But don't forget about the ransom* note.'

---

shack small house, hut
muddling things not doing things right
scream yell, say something very loudly
trapped not free, cannot escape
ransom note in a kidnapping, the note the kidnappers send to get money or goods

Meanwhile, they hear police sirens* and a voice, from outside the shack, says, 'Give up*, you're surrounded!'

The leader* of the gang shouts, 'The Black Hand Gang is never afraid*, but right now we're going to escape!'

'But first let's leave our mark*,' says Eddie, lifting up his dirty* hands.

'Ha, ha, ha! They believed us!' laughs Camilla.

'B-believed what?' ask Wills and Harry together. 'Give up, you're surrounded!'

'See...,' explains Camilla, 'I used the machine...'

... 'Do-It-Yourself-Sounds,' finishes Wills. 'I think it's one of my best inventions!'

'Speaking of inventions...,' asks Harry, 'it's obvious that the gang wanted your pen, but where* on earth did you hide it?'

'Like I told the gang. The hiding place is very close to me!'

sirens alarm signals for the police, fire brigade or ambulance
give up, you're surrounded we're all around you, you can't escape
leader boss
afraid frightened, scared
mark sign
dirty not clean
where on earth where is the pen, it must be a good hiding place

'Here it is!' smiles Wills as he shows the twins where he is hiding the pen.

'In your bow-tie! That's brilliant!' exclaim Harry and Camilla together.

'Is it true that it solves maths problems all* by itself?' asks Camilla.

'Of course! And it's really precise. No more notes* or scribbles... great isn't it? Look at how it solves these maths games.'

Now you try. Which number is missing?

4   16   8   64   ....

Can you get zero by adding, multiplying and dividing the numbers below?

35   65   50   0

---

all by itself completely alone
notes or scribbles writing to work out a problem on paper

After-reading Activities

Reading

1 **Put the sentences in the correct order based on Chapter 4. The first is already given.**

A ☑ Camilla and Harry decide to go to the park to look for Wills.

B ☐ The twins rescue Wills.

C ☐ They hear Wills' voice.

D ☐ They hear a police siren.

E ☐ Camilla talks about the Thousand-tastes-chewing-gum.

F ☐ Harry goes into the shack and finds Wills with the Black Hand Gang.

G ☐ Harry has an idea.

H ☐ The Thousand-tastes-chewing-gum gun makes a huge bubble which becomes a balloon!

Grammar

2 **Complete the sentences with the correct names.**

The Leader of the gang is never afraid.

1 .... has dirty hands and kidnaps kids.

2 .... invents interesting things.

3 .... is a great friend and a good brother.

4 .... is a happy girl and an excellent sister.

5 .... is wearing a bow-tie.

3 **Match the two halves of the sentences.**

	⌐f⌐ Wills' hiding place	**a**	We've solved the case!
1	☐ Eureka!	**b**	me your disgusting
2	☐ Wills is here,		chewing-gum.
3	☐ Please give	**c**	is holding the balloon.
4	☐ I can't remember	**d**	you're surrounded!
	which rope	**e**	but how can we get him
5	☐ Give up,		out?
		~~f~~	is in the forest.

Before-reading Activities

Prediction

4 **Tick (✓) what you think is going to happen.**

		YES	NO
	Wills wins a prize for his pen invention.	☐	☑
1	Wills invents a special pen for English.	☐	☐
2	Camilla invents a new kind of paint.	☐	☐
3	The kids go on holiday together.	☐	☐
4	The parents want them to go to the park.	☐	☐
5	The kids find a new problem to solve.	☐	☐

5 **Compare your answers with a partner. Do you agree about what's going to happen?**

6 **Write how many syllables 1, 2 or 3 in the words. Guess and listen to the chapter to check.**

☐1☐ pen	☐ invention	☐ maths
☐ scribbles	☐ wonderful	☐ prize
☐ bow-tie	☐ ride	☐ beautiful
☐ kids	☐ together	☐ sad
☐ homework	☐ afternoon	☐ problem
☐ happening	☐ bikes	☐ watching

Chapter 5

The Mystery is Solved

▶ 6 'I'm very proud* of my pen,' continues Wills, 'it's a great invention, isn't it?'

'A wonderful one! You're going to win the prize. I'm sure of it!' replies Harry.

'Why don't you invent a pen for English?' suggests Camilla. 'Then I can do all my homework and have the afternoon free!'

'Great idea! Go on, Wills,' agrees Harry.

While we're waiting for Wills' English pen, read the list and find the opposites of the adjectives in the wordsearch.

☐ hot
☐ white
☐ high
☐ large
☐ long
☐ sad
☐ fast
☐ ugly
☐ wet

C	O	L	D	J	E	H	G	B
A	V	R	M	K	M	P	S	L
U	Y	O	L	L	A	M	L	A
S	H	O	R	T	A	I	O	C
S	P	W	O	L	L	S	W	K
R	P	X	L	C	T	Y	L	E
B	E	A	U	T	I	F	U	L
H	A	P	P	Y	A	T	W	B
Y	X	I	W	V	G	U	D	E

proud happy about it

'There you are! Look! Your anti-mud*-sensor is a mess!'

'Oh! I see. It's still not working,' replies Wills, while he looks at his friend's shoes. 'They're all covered in mud.'

'I know what the problem is. Don't worry, I can mend it now.'

'Woof, woof, bow-wow.'

'B-but, what's happening now!' stutters Wills.

'Sit, Rover! Stop running! Stop jumping! It's because of your invention, Super-Supper. He loves it and it gives him so much energy.'

'Watch* out Wills! The pen!' yells Harry.

'Oh no! Now we have to do our homework!' says Camilla.

'My invention!' exclaims Wills.

'Can't you make another one?' asks Harry.

'It takes too much time. I want to enjoy my holidays!'

'Oh no! Now we have to start our summer homework!' says Camilla.

mud dirt and water mixed, makes your clothes dirty
watch out be careful

Tired and a little sad, the kids go to Wills' house.

'Oh, hello kids. There you are,' say his parents as they go into the living room.

'Hi mum, hi dad,' replies Wills.

'How come you're watching television? It's a beautiful day. Why don't you go out? Go for a walk, or ride your bikes,' suggests★ his mum.

'Why don't you go to the park?' suggests Wills' dad.

'Oh no!' groan★ the kids together.

suggests gives an idea
groan say with an unhappy voice

Can you make a pen like Wills'? Put the pictures in order.

1 Draw up the plans.
2 Get the things you need.
3 Assemble the pieces.
4 Register the patent.
5 Present the invention.

Reading

1 Complete the summary of chapter 5. Choose from A, B or C.

After Harry and Camilla ...*rescue*... rescue Wills from the Black Hand Gang, Wills shows them his pen. He put it in (1) .... bow-tie! The special pen solves (2) .... problems all by itself. Wills is very proud (3) .... his pen because it's a great invention. The kids (4) .... to start their summer homework. They go to Wills' house. It's a beautiful day. Wills' parents tell the kids to ride (5) .... bikes to the park. The kids really don't want to go back there!

	A	B	C
	A help	B (rescue)	C go
1	A his	B her	C its
2	A number	B maths	C equation
3	A in	B at	C of
4	A must	B have	C should
5	A them	B our	C their

2 Tick (✓) the sentences true (T) or false (F).

		T	F
	Camilla wants an invention to help her with English.	✓	☐
1	The anti-mud-sensor is not working.	☐	☐
2	The pen breaks.	☐	☐
3	Wills wants to invent lots of things in the holidays.	☐	☐
4	It's a horrible rainy day.	☐	☐
5	Wills' mum and dad are in the living room.	☐	☐

3 Choose the correct verb for these phrases. Be careful! There's one extra!

| ~~go~~ | decide | make | think | stay | enjoy | spend |

...*go*...
home
on holiday
to school

1 ....
what to do
to study maths
where to go

2 ....
hard
about the problem
of something

3 ....
money
time
my free time riding my bike

4 ....
at a hotel
here
for two weeks

5 ....
a plan
a mistake
a sound

Speaking

4 a Wills invented a pen for solving maths problems. Now it's your turn to be an inventor. Work in pairs to invent your own special pen. Think about these things:
- name
- use
- materials
- cost
- special features

4 b Present your ideas to the class.

Great Inventions

A close up look at a few of the inventions that have improved our lives.

The Zipper

Your jeans have one. Your school bag has one. Your jacket probably has one. All these things have zips. Can you imagine life without zips? Every time you undo* a zip, say 'thank you' to a man called Gideon Sundback. He was a Swedish scientist, but he worked in America. In 1917 he patented his special invention for closing things. In 1925, the invention was named 'zipper', because of the zzz-sound it made. Americans still use the word 'zipper', but the British say 'zip'. It's also a verb, remember this next time you zip up, or unzip, your jeans!

How many things with a zip can you think of?

The Plaster

A lot of people invent things to make their everyday lives better. Earle Dickson was one of these people. He worked for an American company, Johnson & Johnson. They made bandages* and other medical products. Mr Dickson's 1921 invention changed our lives. It also made a lot of money for his company. What did he invent? The plaster. Where did his idea come from? His wife.

Mrs Dickson often cut herself when she was cooking. It was very difficult to keep the cuts clean. She always needed someone to help her put on a bandage. Mr Dickson's idea was to stick cotton to a sticky bandage. This way, Mrs Dickson could keep the cut clean and she didn't need anyone to help her. Mr Dickson told his bosses about his idea. They decided to produce plasters. They sold millions and millions. Mr Dickson became vice-president of the company.

to undo to open something
a bandage cotton you use to cover a cut
to text to send an SMS message

The Computer

How much do you know about the history of computers? Did you know that the first computer was made in 87 BC? It was probably made on the island of Rhodes, in Greece. The computer made calculations about stars, planets and the calendar. Of course, it didn't use electricity. And, how much do you know about the history of software? Did you know that people used software to programme machines in ancient China? These machines made cloth by repeating patterns again and again. Centuries later, scientists in Germany, the USA and the UK invented the first modern computers. They were enormous. A computer called ENIAC, developed in America, was as big as a flat. It was a 180 m^2, thirty tonne monster! And it only made 300 calculations a second.

When the first microprocessor was invented in 1971, computers became smaller, cheaper and faster. IBM produced the first personal computers, in the USA.

Today, computers are very small. There are computers everywhere, in cars, in homes, in toys and in schools.

The Mobile Phone

Do you have a mobile phone? Do you text*? Today, it's difficult to imagine life without a mobile. The history of mobile phones is similar to the history of the computer. People wanted mobile technology to improve life, but the first mobiles were very big. They were too big to put in your pocket. In the 1980s, companies in America, Scandinavia and Japan worked to make them smaller and to make the technology better. They also worked to provide mobile networks. Just think - almost nobody had a mobile in 1990. Today, millions and millions of people use them.

A Very Royal Park!

The Regent's Park

London is one of the world's biggest capital cities. It's very busy, but it's also very green. In the middle of this city, you can find some of Britain's most beautiful parks. Both Londoners and tourists love these parks. The Regent's Park is one of London's most popular tourist attractions. There's so much to see and do in the park. Visitors can see formal gardens, a lake, an open-air theatre, London zoo, the London Central Mosque* and much more. A lot of people go to the park to do sport, to go for a walk or to have a picnic.

The History

Today, the park belongs to the Crown. In the past, it belonged to the church. It was part of an abbey*. King Henry VIII closed all the abbeys and monasteries in the 1530s. He decided to keep this land for hunting*. In 1811, the Prince Regent decided to redesign the area. He was very interested in architecture and design. His architects built villas and planned the gardens. The prince's wanted to make London more beautiful. In 1845, The Regent's Park opened to the public. It soon became a very popular place to visit.

The Zoo

A lot of visitors to The Regent's Park go to London Zoo. It's the oldest scientific zoo in the world. The zoo opened to the public in 1847. In the past, London Zoo had a lot of large animals. Today, it's much more modern. The larger animals are in a different zoo, because rhinos and elephants need a lot of space.

Today, the zoo has a theme for the different areas. For example, you can do an 'African Bird Safari' or you can 'Meet the Monkeys'. Did you see the film 'Harry Potter and the Philosopher's Stone'? If you saw it, you probably remember Harry talking to a snake. They filmed this scene in the Reptile House at London Zoo. The animals are stars, too!

Other Royal Parks

The Regent's Park is not the only Royal Park in London. There are, in fact, eight other Royal Parks. Greenwich Park is probably the most important. It's a World Heritage Site. This is because the Prime Meridian Line goes through the park. This is the line of 0° longitude. Many visitors also go to Hyde Park. When the Queen leaves Buckingham Palace on state occasions, she travels along the Mall. This long, straight road goes through St. James's Park from the palace to the centre of London. People who like children's stories go to visit the statue of Peter Pan in Kensington Gardens. People who prefer long walks go to Richmond Park, the largest Royal Park.

a mosque a religious place for Muslims
an abbey a monastery
hunting killing animals for sport

Test yourself

**1 This is the beginning of *In Search of a Missing Friend*.
Find and correct the 9 mistakes.**

It's a horrible, rainy day in London. The twins are in the garden.
Harry is mending his dad's bicycle and Camilla is busy with her
favourite hobby, listening to music. 'Finished! Now my bike is
ready. Camilla, let's go for a ride! Camilla! Camilla? Why are you so
happy? What's wrong?' 'Look! They can't sit still for one second!
Now look what's happened!' Suddenly, they hear a telephone
ringing. They look to see where it's coming from. They see some
cars coming down the road. They're not in a hurry. 'Look! That's
my side-bike,' says Harry. 'And he's not pedalling!' replies Camilla,
'Strange, very strange!'

....

....

....

2 Who said each of the following sentences?

Wills   Camilla   ~~Harry~~   Wills' dad
the shopkeeper at Giant's   the Gang

'Camilla, hurry, we have to find Wills!'
Harry..

1 'Confess or else...'

....

2 'Why don't you go to the park?'

....

3 'We'll never get there before they do.'

....

4 'Today's sale is gigantic!'

....

5 'I'm very proud of my pen.'

....

Syllabus

Vocabulary areas
Friends and enemies
Family and community members
Places
Problem solving
Describing places

Verb tenses and patterns
Present simple
Present continuous
Past simple
Question words
Adjectives
Verb collocation

Teen ⊟ Readers

Stage 1
Maureen Simpson, *In Search of a Missing Friend*
Charles Dickens, *Oliver Twist*

Stage 2
Maria Luisa Banfi, *A Faraway World*
Maria Luisa Banfi, *Francesca's Love*
Maria Luisa Banfi, *The Darnley Family's Long-Lost Necklace*

Stage 3
Mary Flagan, *The Egyptian Souvenir*
Mary Flagan, *Val's Diary*
Maureen Simpson, *Destination: Karminia*
Mark Twain, *The Adventures of Huckleberry Finn*